Exceeding Client Expectations

Mastering Service Excellence in Client-Facing Environments

The Essentials

———————— Business Book ————————

By Jochen De Peuter

INTRODUCTION

In today's highly competitive marketplace, businesses are no longer defined solely by the products they offer but by the quality of the service experiences they provide. Service excellence has emerged as a critical differentiator, shaping client perceptions, fostering loyalty and driving business success.

The evolution of client expectations, fueled by rapid technological advancements and the proliferation of information, has elevated the standards for service delivery. Clients now demand more than just transactional interactions; they seek memorable experiences that resonate on a personal level. This shift necessitates a profound understanding of what makes service exceptional or 'service excellence' and how it can be consistently delivered across all client touchpoints.

The book, "Exceeding Client Expectations: Mastering Service Excellence in Client-Facing Environments", delves into the essence of service excellence, exploring its fundamental principles and illustrating its pivotal role in creating lasting client relationships. It uncovers the theory, strategies and best practices that enable businesses to not only meet but exceed client expectations in client-facing environments and across industries. The book outlines the ingredients of service excellence in a practical manner.

Service excellence is not merely a goal but a journey, one that requires a commitment to continuous improvement, empathy and innovation. By embracing this journey, businesses can transform client interactions into opportunities for building trust and loyalty, ultimately achieving sustainable business growth and a competitive edge.

Enjoy your read as you explore the multifaceted world of service excellence, from understanding your client and defining service quality to leveraging key principles and frameworks like SERVQUAL, 3-P model or others. Whether you're a seasoned professional or new to the field, this business book will equip you with the knowledge and tools necessary to elevate your service standards and thrive in today's dynamic business environment.

ABOUT THE WRITER

Jochen De Peuter is a management consultant who has been working in the past at EHL Advisory Services, part of the EHL Group (Ecole Hôtelière de Lausanne) in Switzerland. He has built extensive know-how and professional experience in the hotel industry and in designing client experiences across industries and has worked on projects globally for large organizations operating in a client-facing environment such as banks, airlines, hotels, retail, healthcare, automotive and FMCG, with a focus on the high-end luxury segment. In addition, he has worked for governmental bodies and private investors.

His approach focuses on placing the client at the center of all strategies, emphasizing the importance of digital transformation, constant innovation and employee education. He regularly publishes online articles on topics such as the role of service excellence in the hospitality industry, creating a culture of service excellence, do's and don'ts to respond to client complaints, contemporary challenges of the client journey in the luxury industry; hereby providing valuable insights into how organizations can adapt and thrive in a rapidly changing environment.

The book has been written in a concise and straightforward manner to help organizations better understand how to build memorable client experiences.

TABLE OF CONTENT

CHAPTER 1 : UNDERSTANDING SERVICE EXCELLENCE Page 6 -14
1. Defining Service Excellence
2. Ingredients Of Success
3. Moments Of Truth
4. Measuring Service Quality

CHAPTER 2 : BUILDING A SERVICE -ORIENTED CULTURE Page 15 -21
1. Living Core Values
2. Leadership's Role
3. Employee Engagement And Empowerment
4. '3-P Model'
5. Service Profit Chain
6. Building Brand Value

CHAPTER 3 : CLIENT RELATIONSHIP MANAGEMENT Page 22 -31
1. Buyer Personas
2. Transmitting And Capturing A Message
3. Building Long-Term Client Relationships
4. Building Communities

CHAPTER 4 : TRAINING AND DEVELOPMENT Page 32 -38
1. Designing Effective Training Programs
2. Continuous Learning And Develoment
3. Measuring Training Success
4. Art Of Being Yourself
5. HR Cycle

TABLE OF CONTENT

CHAPTER 5 : DEVELOPING OPERATING PROCEDURES Page 39 -46

1. Standard Operating Procedures (SOP's)
2. Example Of Standard Operating Procedure

CHAPTER 6 : MANAGING COMPLAINTS Page 47 -53

1. Managing Complaints
2. L-E-A-R-N Method
3. The Don'ts With Complaints
4. Conflict Resolution
5. The Service Recovery Paradox

CHAPTER 7 : THE FUTURE OF SERVICE EXCELLENCE Page 54 -58

1. Emerging Trends In Service Excellence
2. Preparing The Digital Future Of Service Excellence

CHAPTER 8 : BEST PRACTISES Page 59 -67

1. Concrete Examples
2. Selection Of Professional Experiences

CHAPTER 9 : FINAL WORDS Page 68 -70

REFERENCES Page 71 -72

CHAPTER I: UNDERSTANDING SERVICE EXCELLENCE

1.1 Defining Service Excellence

What is service excellence? Service excellence is the consistent delivery of superior service that meets or exceeds client expectations. Service excellence creates positive interactions that foster client loyalty and satisfaction. To define it further, let's break it down into five core components:

1. Consistency - Consistency in service means delivering the same high standard every time a client interacts with a brand. It's crucial because inconsistency can erode trust, while maintaining **trust** is essential. Consistency involves having clear service standards, procedures, training employees thoroughly and continually monitoring performance.

2. Reliability - Reliability is about doing what you say you will do, when you say you will do it. It's one of the most critical factors in building trust and loyalty. Reliable service providers ensure that promises made are **promises kept**, whether it's delivering a product on time or resolving a client issue promptly.

3. Responsiveness - Responsiveness refers to how quickly and effectively you respond to client inquiries and issues. It's about being accessible and **proactive**. Excellent service providers anticipate client needs and are quick to address solutions to any problems that arise.

4. Empathy - Empathy involves understanding and addressing the emotional needs of your clients. It's about showing that you care and value their interests. Empathetic service requires active listening, personalized interactions, creativity, mastery of arts, involving dreams and a genuine concern for the **client's well-being**.

5. Assurance - Assurance is the confidence and trust that your clients place in you. It's built through professional, knowledgeable and courteous interactions. Assurance often stems from a company's reputation, the **competence** of its employees and its commitment to quality.

CHAPTER I: UNDERSTANDING SERVICE EXCELLENCE

1.2 Ingredients of Success

Service Excellence is rooted in five key principles that guide how interactions with clients should be managed. These four key principles are the ingredients to success that ensure that the client touchpoints are a delight and we may speak of service excellence. Every key principle can be further chunked down to a deeper level of detail, containing more sub-elements.

Client-centric culture means putting the client at the heart of everything you do. This involves understanding their needs, preferences and feedback to tailor your services accordingly. It's about creating value for the client and ensuring their experience is seamless and enjoyable. Remember Steve Jobs quoting: "You've got to start with the client experience and work back toward the technology - not the other way around.". To provide excellent service, client-centricity should be unambiguously the lifestyle DNA of the organization.

Quality in service delivery is non-negotiable. This means providing products and services that meet high standards consistently. Quality assurance processes, continuous improvement programs and attention to detail are crucial in maintaining and enhancing service quality. If you position your organization in a high-end market, the infrastructure, products, equipment must show that. Quality implies a great product, with an exceptional service.

Effective communication is the backbone of excellent service. It involves being clear, concise and proactive in your interactions. Keeping clients informed, active listening to their concerns and providing timely updates are all part of good communication practices. Effective communication is about active listening what the client desires and knowing how to empathize with them. At the same time, effective communication is as well associated with messaging, delivering the right message content in the best manner.

Flexibility in service delivery means being adaptable to meet the unique needs of each client. This could involve customizing services, being open to feedback and willing to make changes to improve the client experience, service or product. Flexibility shows clients that you value their individuality and go the extra mile. Flexibility implies that service excellence is dynamically evolving and is never a same permanent condition. Personalized products and services, or in limited editions, is no longer a luxury, it is a key principle of service excellence.

CHAPTER I: UNDERSTANDING SERVICE EXCELLENCE

1.3 Moments Of Truth

Client-facing environments are built out of touchpoints where direct interaction between clients and service providers occurs. These are the **'moments of truth'** where organizations fail or prevail when it comes to serving clients. These environments can be physical, like a retail store or service desk; or virtual, like a website or client service hotline.

In **physical environments**, the atmosphere, layout and accessibility play crucial roles. A welcoming, well-organized and easily navigable space enhances the client experience. For instance, a retail store with friendly staff, clear signage and comfortable waiting areas creates a positive impression. A positive atmosphere in client-facing environments sets the tone for positive client interactions. This includes everything from the background music in a store to the tone of language used on billboards. A positive, welcoming atmosphere can make clients feel valued and comfortable which the client will answer back in a reciprocal manner. The atmosphere must go beyond the expectations, meaning basics such as hygiene, cleanliness, functioning equipment, etc. are the non-negotiables that form the basis of the pyramid.

In **virtual environments**, user experience (UX) is paramount. Websites and apps should be intuitive, fast and responsive. Online chat support, easy navigation and comprehensive FAQ sections can significantly improve client satisfaction. For example, an e-commerce site with a straightforward checkout process and readily available client support is likely to leave a positive impression. Integrating technology in client-facing environments can streamline processes and enhance service delivery. This could be in the form of self-service kiosks in retail stores or in hotels, live chat support on websites, AI robots or mobile apps for easy access to services. Technology should be used to complement and enhance human interaction, not replace it. In general, the use of any digital solution enhances the experience in client-facing environments.

CHAPTER I: UNDERSTANDING SERVICE EXCELLENCE

1.3 Moments Of Truth

In my own professional experiences with hotels, I have observed that the physical environment was mostly ambient, yet the virtual environment such as a user-friendly reservation module or an inspiring pre-arrival e-mail communication was missing. These are as well moments of truth in a client-facing environment, but still often to be ignored despite living in a digital era. Remember, the chain of client touchpoints is only as strong as its weakest link! Quality is a key element to success and it should be consistent. One bad experience is enough for being overall dissatisfied. If we would consider each client touchpoint individually, an organization could, in manner of speaking, have thousands of touchpoints. Each of them counts because details matter when excelling in service, but **perfectionism is impossible, neither an end goal** in an evolving client-facing context. For example, the Luxury Institute (US) has measured that top experience level brands provide an average of 22 positive experiences for each negative experience, while the 5% lowest performing of brands provide only three positive experiences for each negative experience.

CHAPTER I: UNDERSTANDING SERVICE EXCELLENCE

1.4 Measuring Service Quality

Measuring service quality is essential for understanding how well your services meet client expectations and for identifying areas of improvement. It is a multi-faceted process that involves both quantitative and qualitative methods. By utilizing a combination of SERVQUAL, CSAT, NPS, CES, mystery shopping, social media monitoring, employee feedback and service quality indicators, businesses can gain a comprehensive understanding of their service performance according to the strategic goals. These insights enable continuous improvement, leading to higher client satisfaction and loyalty. Hereby, important to know is that service excellence is not defined by a scorecard or achievement of a specific performance indicator; the point of measuring service quality is to **endlessly improve and innovate** the business. Measuring service quality is an agile methodology to test, fail and adapt and should enhance the ownership of the respective managers or heads of departments.

For example, most banks use Net Promotor Score (NPS) as a client satisfaction performance indicator. General metrics such as NPS, at a company level, do not highlight issues in specific parts of the client journey. Therefore, measurements must be sufficiently frequent to identify patterns in client engagement and must go into deeper granularity to get an accurate picture of how client service is performing at crucial and specific interactions during the entire client journey. For that reason, service quality needs to be linked to departmental and managerial accountability.

Depending on the situation, the needs and the market practices, the measurement of service quality varies. Here are the key approaches:

CHAPTER I: UNDERSTANDING SERVICE EXCELLENCE

1.4 Measuring Service Quality

SERVQUAL Model

The SERVQUAL model is one of the most widely used frameworks for measuring service quality. It uses a structured questionnaire to capture, based on scores, client expectations and perceptions for each dimension assessed. Based on the result a gap analysis is made. A higher gap indicates an area needing improvement. The SERVQUAL model is a first step and requires a deeper qualitative analysis in a second step. SERVQUAL assesses service quality based on the following five dimensions. Note hereby the similarity to the five core components of defining service excellence: consistency, reliability, assurance, empathy, responsiveness.

- Tangibles: Physical facilities, equipment and appearance of personnel.
- Reliability: Ability to perform the promised service dependably and accurately.
- Responsiveness: Willingness to help clients and provide prompt service.
- Assurance: Knowledge and courtesy of employees and their ability to inspire trust.
- Empathy: Caring, individualized attention the firm provides its clients.

Client Satisfaction Surveys (CSAT)

Client Satisfaction (CSAT) surveys are simple tools that measure how satisfied clients are with a particular service or interaction. After a service interaction, a client is asked to rate the satisfaction on a scale (e.g., 1-10). The average satisfaction score gauges the overall client satisfaction levels. In a potential next step, open-ended questions gather qualitative feedback for deeper insights.

Net Promotor Score (NPS)

Net Promotor Score (NPS) measures client loyalty by asking clients how likely they are to recommend your service to friends, business partners or colleagues, on a scale of 0-10. Subtract the percentage of Detractors (score 0-6) from the percentage of Promotors (9-10) and you get a result. The NPS score can range from -100 to +100. In the next step, a follow up with both Promotors and Detractors is initiated to understand the reasons behind their scores and to identify areas for improvement. The NPS score is a more spread performance indicator and therefor as well used to benchmark between organizations within a same industry. It is a common client satisfaction KPI in banking industry and financial services.

CHAPTER I: UNDERSTANDING SERVICE EXCELLENCE

1.4 Measuring Service Quality

Several studies show, which I have personally observed during my consulting missions with banks, the positive correlation between the NPS and profitability ratios (Return on Assets). Here is an illustrative overview of the NPS scores in 2023 for some major banks.

Bank / NPS Score (Source: Clientgauge benchmarks)

- First Republic Bank (JP Morgen Chase now) + 72
- First Direct + 66
- ING Luxembourg + 63
- American Express Bank + 52
- Royal Bank of Scotland + 51
- JP Morgan Bank + 31
- Santander UK Bank + 27
- Morgan Stanley + 16
- Westpac - 7

Client Effort Score (CES)

Client Effort Score (CES) measures how easy it is for clients to get their issues resolved or obtain the service they need. A potential question could be: "How easy was it to get your issue resolved today?" with responses typically ranging from "Very Difficult" to "Very Easy." In contrary to the CSAT, the CES specifically calculates the average effort score to understand the ease of service interactions with the aim to identify pain points that cause high effort and streamline processes to reduce client effort.

Mystery Shopping

Mystery shopping involves hiring individuals or industry professionals to act as clients and to evaluate the service received. Mystery shopping is often used by premium and luxury brands with a high level of service standards that are set out by the brand. Examples include luxury retail, car dealerships, gastronomic restaurants or luxury hotels. Mystery visits include scenarios and checklists with very specific moments to verify. The feedback is a combination of a scorecard, to measure adherence to the standards and qualitive feedback, to understand fully the strengths and weaknesses in service delivery with the help of explanations.

CHAPTER I: UNDERSTANDING SERVICE EXCELLENCE

1.4 Measuring Service Quality

Employee Feedback

Employees who interact directly with clients can provide valuable insights into service quality. This can be structured with regular surveys or feedback sessions with frontline employees. In hotels, each guest is asked out of courtesy and practical feedback upon check-out: "How did you enjoy your stay?" "Did everything went well?' The guest's answer could reveal information to directly improve the hotel operations or avoid repetitive service failures such as technical defects, noise issues, cleaning complains, etc. Therefore organizations acting directly with clients (banks, hotels, restaurants, airlines, etc.) should encourage employees to register valuable information from clients into a system so it can be reviewed internally by the upper management. In my professional experience, I have observed in various organizations that the feedback of the ground force is not considered in a structured manner: ivory towers really exist. A bottom up, rather than top-down communication structure is essential to make employee feedback work.

Online review platforms

Online review platforms play an important role in transparent markets, particularly the B2C market. Some examples of review platforms are Google reviews, Tripadvisor, Booking.com or social media platforms. Online reviews are publicly visible client satisfaction indicators and are even more important due to the transparency. As an example, out of my experience in the hotel industry, hotels having above 9/10 review score on Booking.com can request an extra premium price of about +10% compared who have lower scores. Quality sells, especially when genuinely endorsed by other clients. The truth on the strengths and weaknesses lays in the recurrence of specific online feedback. If done in a systematic, structured and highly professional manner, organizations could engage, react online to the client feedback.

Service Quality Indicators

Service Quality Indicators can be measured as part of a specific Service Level Agreement (SLA) that an organization guarantees to its clients. For example, 99% of the calls are answered within 5 minutes. As such, any Key Performance Indicators (KPIs) related to service quality could be measured, depending on the relevance and need. Some examples are:

CHAPTER I: UNDERSTANDING SERVICE EXCELLENCE

1.4 Measuring Service Quality

- Resolution Time: Time taken to resolve client issues.
- Client Retention Rate: Percentage of clients who continue to use your service.
- First Contact Resolution (FCR): Percentage of issues resolved on the first contact.
- Average Response Time: Time taken to respond to client inquiries.

Overview

Tool Name	Method	Focus	Result
SERVQUAL	Qualitative analyis by questionnaires	360° view	Identify gaps to improve
Client Satisfaction Surveys (CSAT)	Score after service	Focus on specific aspect	Qualitative feedback for deeper insights
Net Promotor Score (NPS)	Promotors minus Detractors	Recommendation to others	Score -100 to +100
Client Effort Score (CES)	Question: How easy was it?	Improve ease of service interactions	Identify frictions and pain points
Mystery Shopping	Visit by industry expert	Qualitative feedback	An opinion
Online reviews	Social media and platforms	Averages	Affirmation
Employee feedback	Bottom-up feedback	Qualitative feedback	Call to action
Service quality indicators	Specific to KPI's	SLA's or targets	Company performance

CHAPTER II: BUILDING A SERVICE-ORIENTED CULTURE

2.1 Living Core Values

According to a study by McKinsey, 71% of buying experiences are based on how clients feel they are being treated, meaning a large percentage of business success stems from how a client is treated. Therefore, creating a culture that prioritizes service excellence is crucial for any organization that interacts with clients. The prioritization should be none ambiguous compared to other goals such as shareholder value or profits. A service-oriented culture is the foundation upon which every client interaction is built, ensuring that the organization not only meets but exceeds client expectations.

The (corporate) core values are the guiding principles that dictate behavior and action within an organization. They provide and communicate a common framework and clear understanding that all employees can align with and foster a service-oriented culture. Therefore, determining the fundamental principles or values of an organization are crucial for delivering an exceptional service. Some example core values might be integrity, respect, empathy, care or innovation.

The key challenge is to involve the employees, meaning engaging employees at all levels in the process of adhering to the core values, to ensure the buy-in and give relevance. Living the core values requires regular rehearsal, trainings, clear communication in a written form, as well a clear organizational top-down adherence to these core values. Ultimately the core values get embedded in daily operations and processes, should become part of the companies DNA, even the employees' personality and that into every aspect of the business: from hiring practices to performance evaluations and client interactions.

A good example of a company living up to its core values is Zappos (Book, Zappos Experience by Joseph A. Michelli). Zappos, an online shoe and clothing retailer, is renowned for its strong service-oriented culture. The company's core values, which include delivering WOW through service and include building open and honest relationships, are integral part to its business model and are reflected in every client interaction. The company holds a unique and special 'Zapponian' subculture with uncommon practices that drive the client experience and make the employee feel part of a likeminded family.

CHAPTER II: BUILDING A SERVICE-ORIENTED CULTURE

2.2 Leadership's Role

Business leaders, read as the senior management, play a pivotal role in shaping and sustaining a culture of service excellence. Their vision, actions and attitudes set the tone for the entire organization and are key to a sincere client-oriented culture. For example, when Howard Schultz returned as CEO of Starbucks in 2008 to restore the company's profitability, he implemented several key strategies aimed at enhancing the customer experience including improving the quality of products and services and refining the overall customer experience. At the end, what clients want is a great Starbucks coffee experience in return for a premium price. In that perspective, it is in my opinion that a top-down inspirational leadership's role is the basic layer to master service excellence in a client facing environment.

Leaders must **lead by example**. Leaders must embody the core values and service standards they wish to see in their teams. This includes demonstrating a commitment to client satisfaction and going above and beyond to meet client needs. They should pick the words very careful as they are providing the vision and direction. A clear communication of the organization's vision and how each employee contributes to service excellence is crucial. Leaders should articulate the importance of client-centric strategies and install clear, achievable goals that relate to client-centricity. Out of my professional experience, I have observed that still many organizations focus too much on solely the financial performance indicators.

Ultimately, each employee is as well in the role or a leader. Leadership in service excellence requires empowering employees and giving the responsibility to own success. Leaders should empower their employees by providing the necessary tools, training and autonomy to deliver exceptional service. At the hotel chain Ritz-Carlton, leadership is committed to creating a culture where employees are encouraged to take initiative and make decisions that enhance the guest experience. This empowerment is a key element of their service excellence. For example, they may spend up to 2'000 USD, without any managerial approval, to make a service recovery in case of a service failure for a hotel guest.

CHAPTER II: BUILDING A SERVICE-ORIENTED CULTURE

2.3 Employee Engagement And Empowerment

Engaged and empowered employees are essential for delivering a consistent, high-quality service. When employees feel valued and empowered, they are more likely to take ownership of their roles and go the extra mile for clients. The most common strategies for employee engagement and empowerment are:

1. Training and development: Provide continuous training and development opportunities to enhance employees' skills and knowledge. This could include training on corporate culture or behavior.

2. Recognition and rewards: Recognize and reward employees for their contributions to service excellence. This could include formal awards, bonuses, personal recognitions or making role models.

3. Encouraging autonomy: Allow employees the autonomy to make decisions that benefit the client, fostering a sense of ownership and responsibility. Make the employees feel to be an important part of the overall success.

An industry example for employee engagement and empowerment is Southwest Airlines. Southwest Airlines empowers its employees to deliver exceptional client service by fostering a supportive work environment and encouraging them to make decisions in the best interest of the client. Its strategy includes one of the lowest-priced solutions for air travel, with help of low operating costs due to employee's engagement, flexibility and willingness to go the extra mile. Southwest Airlines are among the most profitable airline companies in the world.

CHAPTER II: BUILDING A SERVICE-ORIENTED CULTURE

2.4 '3-P Model'

The '3-P Model' (People, Process and Product/Physical Evidence) is a framework used to ensure that all aspects of service delivery are aligned with the goal of exceeding client expectations. Its components are

1. People: The individuals who interact with clients, including their skills, attitude and behavior.
2. Process: The procedures and workflows that ensure consistent service delivery.
3. Product: The tangible aspects that clients encounter, such as the physical environment, branding and marketing materials.

The importance of the 3-P model lays in the weight of importance of its' components and the understanding why it is. Imagine a fine-dining restaurant and a McDonald's restaurant. When going to the McDonald's restaurant the value lays on a clean and ambient restaurant area (physical evidence) and a tasty, quick meal and a cheap price (efficient process). In the fine dining restaurant, the bar lays obviously higher. The aim is to be surprised, to have an experience, to be explained what the menu is about, to ask for personalized menus, to taste extraordinary wines, etc. Clearly, only well-trained people with the right attitude and behavior can deliver that kind of service. That is why, while the processes and physical evidence are for granted, the 'people' component is the utmost essential 3-P element when positioning in a top-level service environment. Only exceptional cooks, sommeliers and experienced waiters master the art of delighting high demanding clients. At the same time, neither a McDonald's restaurant would work well without good staff, people. Disney excels in the people component of the 3-P Model. Their cast members (people) are carefully selected and trained to deliver magical experiences to children.

CHAPTER II: BUILDING A SERVICE-ORIENTED CULTURE

2.5 Service Profit Chain

The 3-P model is a great transition to explain the Service Profit Chain, a sexy term for the principle that Virgin Group prioritizes "employees first, clients second and shareholders third". Effectively, in the end shareholders do well when the client and the staff are happy.

The Service Profit Chain is a theory and model that explains how employee satisfaction, client loyalty and profitability are interconnected in service-based businesses. The model suggests that there is a direct link between these elements, creating a chain of cause-and-effect relationships that drive business success in a continuous loop. The Service Profit Chain can be visualized as follows:

Internal Service Quality → Employee Satisfaction → Employee Retention and Productivity → External Service Value → Client Satisfaction → Client & Brand Loyalty → Revenue Growth and Profitability.

By focusing on improving each link in this chain, businesses can create a sustainable cycle of improvement and success. The model emphasizes the importance of investing in employee well-being and service quality as foundational steps toward achieving long-term profitability.

How to explain each step? The Internal Service Quality refers to the quality of the workplace environment, including the tools, resources and support employees receive to perform their jobs effectively. When employees are satisfied with their jobs and can do their work well, they are more likely to be motivated, engaged and productive. This satisfaction comes from good internal service quality, appropriate compensation, opportunities for growth and a positive work culture. Satisfied employees are more likely to stay with the company longer, reducing turnover costs and retaining valuable institutional knowledge. They are also generally more productive and deliver better performance. Productive and engaged employees provide better service to clients, enhancing the perceived value of the service. This includes responsiveness, reliability and the overall quality of interactions with clients. A high service value leads to higher client satisfaction. When clients receive good service, they are more likely to be pleased with their experience and satisfied clients are more likely to become loyal to the brand and continue to do business with the company. They are also more likely to recommend the company to others, creating a positive word-of-mouth effect or positive net promotor score.

CHAPTER II: BUILDING A SERVICE-ORIENTED CULTURE

2.5 Service Profit Chain

Client loyalty translates into repeat business, higher sales and lower acquisition cost of new clients through referrals. This results in revenue growth and increased profitability. With a better profitability, there are more means to invest in the workplace and employees which restarts the process again from the beginning. By focusing on improving each link in this chain, businesses can create a sustainable cycle of improvement and success. At the end, the model emphasizes the importance of investing in employee well-being and service quality as foundational steps toward achieving long-term profitability.

CHAPTER II: BUILDING A SERVICE-ORIENTED CULTURE

2.6 Building Brand Value With Client Experience

In today's competitive marketplace, building brand value is crucial for long-term success. A significant component of this process is the client experience, which encompasses every interaction a client has with a brand. Client experience can be seen as an important part of the service excellence.

Superior client experience can transform a one-time buyer into a loyal client and an advocate for the brand, encourages repeat business and generates positive word-of-mouth. Conversely, a negative experience can lead to client attrition and damage to the brand's reputation. Briefly, the experience influences how clients feel about a brand and their willingness to engage with it in the future.

Client experiences do not always have to be expensive or amazing, they can be original as well. For example, some hotels or bars just create their playlist on Spotify to bring forward their brand or others provide signature services. For example, Mc Donald's provide personalized Happy Meals with a gift for children. The aspect of differentiation is key. In markets where products and services are often similar, bespoke client experiences becomes a key differentiator. As well called **signature services and goods**. People speak about it because it goes beyond the basic expectations and can leave a lasting impression.

McDonald's - Happy Meal with a signature gift for children

Nordstrom - Unquestioned return policy and personal stylists

Starbucks - Customization for the beverages, with occasionally a personal touch

Tesla - Over-the-air software updates for their vehicle

American Express - Premium concierge service for specific card holders

Apple is known for its exceptional products, client service and support, which plays a significant role in its strong brand loyalty and makes the company among the most valuable companies in the world. Apple has built a powerful brand identity with admittedly the most amazing products for sale at premium prices. Building brand value through client experience is a powerful strategy that can lead to a strategic asset.

CHAPTER III: CLIENT RELATIONSHIP MANAGEMENT

3.1 Buyer Personas

Who is your client? Understanding who your client is, forms the bedrock of service excellence. Your client is the recipient of your product or service, but this simple definition belies the complexity inherent in truly knowing them. It's proven that describing and leveraging the profiles of your most typical client types, 'buyer personas', can lead to tangible financial benefits, including increased revenue, higher profitability and reduced client acquisition costs. These advantages are backed by concrete data that can be found online, illustrating the powerful impact of understanding and targeting specific client segments. The better you Know Your Client (KYC), the better you can serve them. Remark that KYC in this context is a service excellence perspective and has nothing to do with compliance rules for banks. A comprehensive understanding of your client from a service perspective involves demographic, psychographic and behavioral insights. Here are the steps you can take to get a clear picture of your client by creating a 'buyer persona'.

First, conduct a market research. Market research happens on a macro- and micro-economic level. **Macro-economic data** comes from existing industry reports and market analysis reports to understand current industry trends and client segments relevant to your business. **Micro-economic data** comes directly from potential clients through sales data, surveys and questionnaires. Ask about their demographics, preferences and behaviors. Gather a small group of potential clients to discuss their needs, preferences and feedback on your product or service. These data can as well be collected out of website analytics such as Google Analytics to track who is visiting your website, their demographics, behavior and how they interact with your site; social media platforms to see who is engaging with your content and what their profiles look like. Sales data identifies who is buying your products or services, including their purchase history and patterns.

CHAPTER III: CLIENT RELATIONSHIP MANAGEMENT

3.1 Buyer Personas

In a second step, based on the aggregated data 'buyer personas' can be created. There are 3 variables in which client profiles are ty. The aim is too be as complete as possible in the description.

- Demographic information provides the basic statistical characteristics of your client. These include age, gender, income, education level, occupation and location. For instance, if you run a high-end boutique, your client might be women aged 30-50 years with a higher income level and a penchant for luxury goods.

- Psychographic information delves into the attitudes, values, interests and lifestyles of your clients. This data is often gleaned through more qualitative methods such as focus groups or social media analysis. For example, our high-end boutique client might value exclusivity, personalized service, attends social events and travels.

- Behavioral insights looks at how clients interact with your product or service. This includes purchase patterns, brand loyalty and product usage. For instance, you might find that your high-end boutique clients frequently purchase new arrivals and prefer in-store shopping experiences for the personal touch.

Example: "Sophia, the Fashionista"

Sophia Monroe is a 28-year-old woman living in Paris. She works as a Marketing Manager at a creative agency and earns an annual net income of €40,000. Sophia has a Bachelor's Degree in Fashion Marketing, which aligns with her passion for fashion. She is single and enjoys a vibrant social life, often attending events and networking within the fashion industry.

Sophia is a confident and assertive individual who takes pride in her unique and eclectic style. She is known for mixing contemporary designer pieces with vintage finds, creating a look that is both chic and distinctive. Sophia is also creative and enjoys experimenting with bold fashion choices, often making a statement with unique accessories.

CHAPTER III: CLIENT RELATIONSHIP MANAGEMENT

3.1 Buyer Personas

In her free time, Sophia loves fashion blogging, attending fashion shows and shopping. She also enjoys traveling and practicing yoga. As a tech-savvy individual, she is very comfortable with online shopping and is active on social media platforms like Instagram, TikTok and Pinterest. These platforms are not only a source of inspiration for her but also a space where she shares her own style and influences others.

Sophia has a keen interest in the latest fashion trends, designer collections and sustainable fashion. She is particularly drawn to high-end brands such as Louis-Vuitton and Gucci, but she also appreciates more accessible brands like Zara. Additionally, she loves hunting for unique pieces in thrift stores.

When it comes to shopping, Sophia prefers a mix of online and in-store experiences. She enjoys browsing luxury department stores and trendy boutiques, but she also values the convenience and variety offered by online shopping. However, the abundance of choices available can sometimes overwhelm her, making it challenging to keep up with the latest trends and collections.

Sophia is motivated by her desire to be a trendsetter and influence others' fashion choices. She seeks high-quality pieces that reflect her personality and is increasingly interested in sustainable fashion. However, balancing her passion for luxury items with financial prudence is a challenge she faces, as is finding stylish and sustainable options that meet her high standards.

When making purchasing decisions, Sophia extensively researches new trends, reads fashion blogs and watches runway shows online. She is influenced by fashion influencers, celebrity styles and editorial content. Often, she seeks second opinions from friends or followers on social media before making a purchase.

Sophia's primary goal is to continuously refine and evolve her personal style. She strives to stay ahead of fashion trends and enjoys being the first to showcase new looks. As she becomes more conscious of environmental issues, she is also increasingly focused on incorporating sustainable choices into her wardrobe.

CHAPTER III: CLIENT RELATIONSHIP MANAGEMENT

3.2 Transmitting And Capturing A Message

Effective communication is a key principle for mastering service excellence in client-facing environments. By truly understanding client needs, utilizing effective communication strategies, respecting cultural differences and fostering long-term relationships and communities, businesses can exceed expectations and build lasting client loyalty. That is why Client Relationship Management includes transmitting and capturing the right message. Transmitting and capturing a message correctly when speaking or listening is not a given! The message you are saying is not necessarily what the counterparty is receiving. Secondly a simple message contains a **thousand signals**. Communication is complex, it contains verbal elements such as tone of voice, speed, confidence and language skills but at the same time nonverbal elements such as appearance, facial expressions, nonverbal cues, eye contact, body smell and clothing.

According to Albert Mehrabian's 7-38-55 communication model, only 7% of the message is conveyed through the words we use in spoken communication, while 38% is through the tone and voice and 55% through the non-verbal elements. For example, a homeless person speaking does not have the same impact as a billionaire speaking even if the words and voice are the same. Another example is lying or deceiving someone: words can lie, but the eyes do not lie. Meaning even without speaking, one already communicates a message. Non-verbal cues can convey as much information as words, sometimes even more. Understanding and utilizing non-verbal communication can enhance client interactions significantly. They are of utmost importance in a client-facing environment. In luxury hospitality, luxury retail and business class on airlines, you often find well-groomed and mostly attractive personnel, trained to use positive body language and smile to create a welcoming atmosphere for guests. For welcoming professions, appearance is key to make a first good impression. Here are some industry-specific examples for luxury retail on non-verbal communication in a client-facing environment:

Positive body language, such as an open posture turned toward the client, nodding and smiling, can make clients feel valued and understood. High-end luxury retail brands train their staff to walk alongside clients turned with their body towards a client when visiting a store, 'the lateral crab-walk', maintaining an open posture while guiding them to the right area simultaneously.

CHAPTER III: CLIENT RELATIONSHIP MANAGEMENT

3.2 Transmitting And Capturing A Message

To understand what a client wants, you need to take the time to understand the whole picture from the speaker's perception. That is what active listening is about. Active listening is more than hearing. It involves a full devotion to what a client is saying and requires full concentration, understanding, reading, interpreting and empathy to capture what a client really means. The true and specific client needs are uncovered by applying question techniques while nodding, smiling and maintaining eye contact to motivate clients to provide more information. Here is how to apply the question techniques in client-facing environments:

1. Open-ended questions encourage clients to share information openly and provide detailed responses. Open-ended questions are ideal for breaking the ice and gathering lots of information, including spontaneous hints at the beginning of the conversation. Open-ended questions provide the most information. For example, "What does your wife like to wear?" or "How can we improve our service to better meet your expectations?" A subcategory of open-ended questions is probing questions, which encourage giving an opinion in a subtle manner. Examples include "Why do you think this is a good product?"

2. Closed-ended questions are useful for obtaining specific information, clarifying, supporting the client, or concluding the deal. They should not be used at the beginning of the conversation but at a more advanced stage. Examples include "Do you prefer red or blue?", "Are you satisfied with your choice?", "Did I summarize correctly?"

Phrasing the Message

Phrasing a message with the right words is key! For example, in the luxury market, across industries, the use of language is very precisely chosen, with sophistication in the wording and the use of adverbs to bring forward the emotional aspects. Luxury is about feelings, expectations and environment, while generic brands are about price and product descriptions. Some typical words used in the luxury segment are: "elegant, rare, timeless, genial, priceless, proud, noble, craftsmanship, perfection, discrete, beloved, prestigious, passionate, sincere, etc". Here are some differences in wording between generic & premium services/products and luxury services/products:

CHAPTER III: CLIENT RELATIONSHIP MANAGEMENT

3.2 Transmitting And Capturing A Message

- Generic: Tangible vs Luxury: Intangible
- Generic: Rational vs Luxury: Emotional
- Generic: Comparative vs Luxury: Superlative
- Generic: Time-framed vs Luxury: Infinite
- Generic: Performant vs Luxury: Unmatched

To illustrate the importance of phrasing, consider inviting your wife for dinner. This can happen in a generic or emotional manner.

The generic version: "Let's go for dinner, I have booked a table in a restaurant at 20:00."

The emotional version: "My dear love, I invite you for dinner at your beloved restaurant. I have booked the best table with a stunning sea view at 20:00 and look forward to celebrating this precious moment of happiness together with you."

Both versions convey the same result, but the choice of words in the second version is more colorful and inspiring. The power of emotions makes the difference. The use of clear, concise and positive language is key in communication, but also the opportunity to bring true delight in the message with emotions around family, peace, time, wealth, timelessness and abstract matters when communicating with clients.

Etiquette

Etiquette applies to social behavior in general and social behavior communicates with clients. For example, an employee in a retail store typing on his or her cellphone may unintentionally offend a client by not giving full attention or immediate support. To avoid these situations, etiquette is designed. Etiquette is a set of unwritten rules designed to close the gap between generations, educational backgrounds, habits, cultures, etc. Etiquette enforces adherence to the company values and desired client expectations.

CHAPTER III: CLIENT RELATIONSHIP MANAGEMENT

3.2 Transmitting And Capturing A Message

Professional etiquette is about politeness, courtesy, mutual respect and professionalism. Etiquette breeds empathy. Examples include greeting clients warmly, using polite language, thanking clients for their time and business, not using cell phones in the presence of clients, being ready to help at any moment, respecting deadlines, communicating any delays proactively, maintaining a professional demeanor in all interactions or maintaining an appropriate email etiquette. Even if common sense for some, training etiquette rules in any client-facing organization is key to communicating the right social behavior. For example, The Ritz-Carlton's motto, "We are Ladies and Gentlemen serving Ladies and Gentlemen," exemplifies their commitment to professional etiquette and exceptional service.

Clients often become loyal because of the personnel serving them, asking back for the same employee for support. Employees in client-facing environments must be able to bond to clients and provide value. That is why etiquette goes beyond the non-verbal or politeness elements. Etiquette demonstrates that the employee is sophisticated, educated and interesting. Truly interesting employees do not speak a thousand times about the weather to their clients. Etiquette is being able to engage in meaningful and interesting stories that could inspire the clients such as details of the product, food recipes, ingredients, but as well about vacations, cultural events, company storyline, sports, actuality or simply how someone is doing.

Remark that etiquette differs from protocols, which refer to the code of conduct for government and international officials. Protocols may transcend the mere obedience to applicable laws and include additional prescriptions for morality, traditional local practices, professional standards, information sharing, etc. For example, French has long held the esteemed position of being the international language of diplomacy. French's grammatical structure and vocabulary offer nuance and elegance, enabling diplomats to convey complex ideas with clarity, allowing representatives from diverse linguistic backgrounds to engage in discussions without biases.

CHAPTER III: CLIENT RELATIONSHIP MANAGEMENT

3.3 Building Long-Term Client Relationships

The client relationship continues in a non-stop manner via newsletters, social media, surveys, publicity, invitations, banners, TV, etc. In that extent, virtual environments have surely intensified and stretched the entire client journey and emphasized the pre-purchase and post-purchase experience. This book does not discuss the marketing effects of the virtual communication channels but focuses on how to excel in client experiences. Fact is, that any client relationship is a non-stop relationship and needs to be nurtured recurrently such as any other relationship. Nurturing long-term relationships with clients is essential. Long-term relationships are built on three pillars: trust, consistency and ongoing engagement. The basics remain to deliver consistent quality and reliability in the service-levels by trust and consistency. Clients should know they can depend on you, this is non-negotiable. Secondly, ongoing engagement to nurture the bond with clients is key to success. Here are some best practices:

Personalization

The proper use of a CRM tool is essential to tailor the approach with the right message. Therefore, design your CRM system not for generalization, nor segmentation but for personalization. Provide solutions specifically tailored to meet individual needs or personal affairs. Show genuine interest in the client's success, track record, personal affairs and well-being. Take the time to understand the specific needs and preferences of each client and track them appropriately in the CRM system. For example, a personalized birthday invitation for a store visit with a goodie bag is a personalized way to reward your clients. A personal phone call or WhatsApp message will prove to be more effective than a lengthy email. Build a personal connection by remembering and tracking important details about each client.

Proactive Engagement

Client relationships are all about proactive communication. In a business relationship, you must be the one who takes the initiative: proactively anticipate client needs and address them before they become issues, schedule regular check-ins to discuss the client's evolving needs or positively impress by speed of resolution for a client request. Proactive engagement will give you credibility and trust. Feedback loops are as well part of the pro-activity. Take time to listen to client feedback and concerns actively and act on feedback to make meaningful improvements.

CHAPTER III: CLIENT RELATIONSHIP MANAGEMENT

3.3 Building Long-Term Client Relationships

Loyalty Programs

Offer loyalty programs or incentives for clients, as well as exclusive offers to the most loyal clients. Clearly distinguish your client's grade, based on actual data. Make your clients feel that they are important to you and part of your organization.

Social Media

Social media has become key to staying connected to your clients. It has become a main platform of communication for most of us. Therefore, provide regular updates. Keep clients informed about progress, changes and updates regularly. Inspire them with great content: online reels, images, videos, etc.

Trust And Transparency

Be honest about what you can deliver and manage expectations realistically, as well be honest to your organizational core principles. Share information openly and avoid hidden fees or terms and bad surprises. Ultimately, consistent trust is a synonym for reliability in your products or services. This is the basis for a solid long-term relationship.

Value Addition

Offer additional value in your communication; don't be invasive with irrelevant or repetitive information. Continuously seek ways to improve and innovate your offerings. Consult through expert advice, resources or extra services. Provide an outstanding client service with effectively well-trained staff.

CHAPTER III: CLIENT RELATIONSHIP MANAGEMENT

3.4 Building Communities

Creating a community around your brand or organization will deepen client relationships and foster loyalty. Some brands have built out strong client communities, such as Porsche, Harley-Davidson or LEGO. For example, LEGO has created an online community where fans can submit their own designs, vote on others' designs and discuss ideas. Successful designs are turned into official LEGO sets, with the original designer receiving a portion of the sales. This community has not only driven engagement but also innovation, as it taps directly into the creativity and passion of LEGO enthusiasts. Porsche has created a global community of fans, organizing constant events, rallies, visits to the Porsche Museum, test drives on circuits, etc. These events are made to meet and socialize with like-minded Porsche fans. Briefly, these organizations have developed social platforms to bring clients together, share knowledge and strengthen the sense of belonging.

Forums where clients can interact with the brand and another position the organization or brand as a **thought industry leader**. These physical events, forums, are further amplified using social media, storytelling. Clients who feel part of a community are more likely to remain loyal to your brand. Communities provide a direct line to client feedback, helping you understand their needs and preferences. Engaged clients often become brand advocates, advocate for your brand during challenging times and spreading positive word-of-mouth. Here are some steps to consider when building a community around your organization:

Above all, understand your clients and identify the common interests and goals that unite your clients and build a theme around it. Create a platform for interaction. Provide physical and virtual spaces where clients can interact such as webinars, workshops, meet-ups, drinks, events, exhibitions, parties, virtual spaces, etc. Promote the content online through blog posts, social media, videos and newsletters. Encourage participation among the members, activate them. Ask questions, create polls and encourage clients to share their experiences and insights. Among those members, identify and empower enthusiastic clients who can act as community leaders. Equip these leaders with the tools and resources they need to foster engagement within the community. Reward participation with generosity as part of the marketing budget. Recognize active community members through shout-outs, badges, or exclusive access to events and exclusive content. Provide incentives to participate.

CHAPTER IV: TRAINING AND DEVELOPMENT

4.1 Designing Effective Training Programs

In the realm of client-facing environments, the quality of service delivered hinges significantly on the skills, knowledge and attitudes of the personnel involved. This chapter delves into the critical aspects of training and development, offering insights into designing effective training programs, fostering continuous learning, measuring training success, leveraging personality insights and recruiting the right candidates. These components are essential in exceeding client expectations and mastering service excellence. Effective training programs are the cornerstone of any successful client-facing organization. They ensure that personnel is well-equipped with the necessary skills and knowledge to meet and exceed client expectations. In a high demanding client-facing environment, **clients expect 'competence'** before they give trust.

Before designing a training program, it is crucial to conduct a thorough needs assessment. This involves identifying the specific skills and knowledge gaps within the team. Methods such as surveys, interviews, performance reviews and client feedback can provide valuable insights into areas that require improvement. Secondly, training programs are not built for the sake of compliance. Training programs must have clear objectives. Training objectives should be specific, measurable, achievable, relevant and time-bound (SMART). Clear objectives guide the development of the training content and provide a benchmark for evaluating the program's effectiveness. For example, improving effective complaint handling and complaint closure by summer with an immediate complaint resolution rate of 95%.

The best training programs are a blend of technical learning and practical doing, the mix enhances learning outcomes. The high engagement by letting the participants do the exercises, leave the most memorable learnings over time. It is beneficial to use a variety of training methods, including classroom sessions, e-learning modules, role-playing and on-the-job training. This diversity caters to different learning styles and keeps participants engaged. One training session should focus on 1-3 key learnings a time, maximum, not more! To consume and apply the learnings requires time, therefore do not engage employees in one after the other training program but leave some weeks or months in between to allow the employees growing in their role. Continuous monitoring during the implementation phase helps to address any issues promptly and ensures that the program stays on track. For the design, external consultants can infuse organizations with new learnings, another view or simply a specific knowledge on one single topic.

CHAPTER IV: TRAINING AND DEVELOPMENT

4.2 Continuous Learning And Development

In a rapidly changing business environment, continuous learning and development are vital. They enable personnel to stay updated with the latest industry trends, technologies and best practices, ensuring that they can consistently deliver high-quality service.

Organizations should foster a culture that values and encourages continuous learning, some organizations even have it as a core value. This can be achieved by promoting curiosity, supporting professional development, spending budget and recognizing and rewarding learning initiatives. Regular training sessions help employees to refine their skills and stay abreast of new developments. Out of experience, I have noted that client-facing organizations such as hotels and luxury retail pay a lot of attention to the role of HR L&D (Human Resources Learning & Development), even for the smaller organizations. It is key to have a dedicated person who is **facilitating the development of employees.**

Beyond specific trainings, it is essential to offer ongoing training opportunities among which advanced courses, certifications, seminars and access to online learning platforms. Encouraging employees to take ownership of their own learning journey can lead to more engaged and motivated personnel. Providing resources such as books, online courses and learning communities can support self-directed learning.

CHAPTER IV: TRAINING AND DEVELOPMENT

4.3 Measuring Training Success

Measuring the success of training programs is essential to ensure they are delivering the desired outcomes and providing a return on investment. Therefor data collection is crucial for evaluating training success. This can be done through surveys, tests, performance assessments and client feedback. Both quantitative and qualitative data provide valuable insights into the effectiveness of the training. Once the data is collected, it needs to be analyzed to identify trends, strengths and areas for improvement. Detailed reports should be prepared and shared with stakeholders, highlighting the training program's impact and suggesting actionable recommendations. Based on the evaluation results, organizations should continuously refine and improve their training programs. This iterative process ensures that training remains relevant, effective and aligned with organizational goals. Here are two key strategies for evaluating training effectiveness:

Setting SMART Objectives

Establishing own clear SMART objectives for evaluating training success is the first step. This could include metrics such as improved performance, increased client satisfaction, reduced error rates, complaints resolution rate and enhanced employee engagement. The objectives are backed by data and depend on the corporate strategy, client feedback or operational effectiveness.

The Kirkpatrick Model

The Kirkpatrick Model is a widely used framework for evaluating training programs. It involves four levels of evaluation: level 1 - reaction, level 2 - learning, level 3 - behavior, and level 4 - results. By assessing these levels, organizations can gain a comprehensive understanding of the training program's impact.

- Level 1 - Reaction: The degree to which participants find the training favorable, engaging, and relevant to their jobs.
- Level 2 - Learning: The degree to which participants acquire the intended knowledge, skills, confidence and commitment based on the participation in the training.
- Level 3 - Behavior: The degree to which participants apply what they learned during the training when there are back on the job
- Level 4 - Results: The degree to which targeted organizational outcomes occur because of the training initiative and subsequent support and accountability package.

CHAPTER IV: TRAINING AND DEVELOPMENT

4.4 Art of Being Yourself

Service leadership in client-facing environments requires more than just technical skills and knowledge. It demands a deep understanding of oneself and the ability to leverage personal strengths to inspire and guide others. Moreover, it is possible to train skills, but a personality cannot be changed and should therefore be cherished and leveraged.

As a first step, it is important to understand your personality. **Self-awareness is the foundation of effective leadership**. Organizations should invest time in understanding their employees' personality traits, strengths and areas for improvement. Tools such as personality assessments e.g., Myers-Briggs Type Indicator, DISC, Insights can provide valuable insights. Unfortunately, it is rarely considered in a hiring process, but it is an essential, genuine, transparent and true instrument for selecting the best profiles for the specific job. For example, the insights discovery model features four main type of characters based on four color codes:

- Blue profile features introvert-rational: person likes to work at own pace, analyzing and solving problems. Ideal in finance, accounting, consulting, research, not ideal in direct client-facing environments.
- Red profile features extravert-rational: person is direct, sets the pace, takes decisions, has lower empathy. Ideal in finance, leadership roles; but not suited in direct client-facing environments.
- Green profile features introvert-emotional: person is people-oriented, empathic, a giver, quiet in groups. Ideal in client-facing environments, medical care, hosting, people- related positions, social influencing.
- Yellow profile features extravert-emotional: person is innovative, creative, loud, procrastinator, extravert. Ideal in client-facing environments, innovations, animation, entertainment, sales roles, social media.

Emotional intelligence (EI) is critical for successful service leadership and for client-facing environments. It involves recognizing and managing one's emotions and understanding and influencing the emotions of others. Employees with high EI can navigate complex interpersonal dynamics, resolve conflicts, be a moral support and foster a positive work environment. For example, take the claims process for an insurance company. If a client has a car accident, he might feel guilty and could look to agents for emotional support. If an insurer is too focused on the resolution and speed, the client might come away with a negative view.

CHAPTER IV: TRAINING AND DEVELOPMENT

4.4 Art of Being Yourself

Therefore, the ideal profiles in a direct client-facing environment are the employees who care about feelings (green-oriented) and who can resolve problems in an innovative manner (yellow-oriented).

Ultimately, the art of thriving in a client facing job and the art of service excellence equals the art of being yourself and not pretending to be. Genuine service leaders are not required to be instructed how to please others; they are **born to do it**. Great service leaders are committed to continuous self-improvement and constantly question themselves. They seek feedback, reflect on their experiences and strive to enhance their service leadership skills. This commitment to personal growth sets a powerful and inspiring example for their teams.

CHAPTER IV: TRAINING AND DEVELOPMENT

4.5 HR Cycle

In a client-facing environment, the role of Human Resources is essential. For example, recruiting the right candidates is essential for building a high-performing team, capable of delivering exceptional client service. The Human Resources cycle encompasses several stages, from attracting talent to onboarding and beyond.

Attracting Talent

Attracting the right talent begins with a compelling employer brand. Organizations should clearly communicate their values, culture and the benefits of working with them. Job postings should be clear, concise and aligned with the desired candidate profile.

Screening and Selection

The screening and selection process should be thorough and objective. This involves reviewing resumes, conducting interviews and assessing candidates' skills, experience and cultural fit. Behavioral interviews and situational judgment tests provide deeper insights into candidates' suitability for client-facing roles and are essential. Remember, skills can be learnt at a later stage. Ideally, the selection is based on the assessment of at least two independent interviewers.

Onboarding and Training

Effective onboarding is crucial for setting new hires up for success. It should include a comprehensive introduction to the organization, induction training to clarify its values and its client service standards. The induction training should equip new employees with the right understanding to excel in their roles. As well, the training of job-specific skills is part of the onboarding process which can run even up to one year after hiring.

Performance Management

Regular performance reviews and feedback are essential for ongoing development. These reviews should be constructive, focusing on strengths and areas for improvement. Clear performance metrics and goals help employees understand expectations and strive for excellence.

CHAPTER IV: TRAINING AND DEVELOPMENT

4.5 HR Cycle

Career Development

Organizations should support employees' career development by offering opportunities for advancement, skill development and leadership training. A clear career path can enhance employee engagement and retention, contributing to a stable and motivated workforce.

Employee Retention

Retaining top talent is critical for maintaining a high level of service excellence. This involves creating a positive work environment, offering competitive compensation and benefits and recognizing and rewarding outstanding performance.

Exit

The employee leaves the company. An exit interview allows you to understand the points of improvement from both sides. Relevant feedback gets integrated in the HR cycle and HR policy.

CHAPTER V: DEVELOPING OPERATING PROCEDURES

5.1 Standard Operating Procedures (SOP's)

Standard Operating Procedures (SOPs) are the backbone of consistent and high-quality service delivery. They provide clear guidelines for performing tasks and delivering services, ensuring that every team member knows what is expected of them. Standard Operating Procedures are designed to facilitate and elevate the interaction with clients, to reduce mistakes and to optimize internal workflows.

Each important touchpoint along the client journey is subject to a detailed engineering process aimed at creating positive client experiences. Developing SOPs requires time, several trials and, above all, **internal support from the primary users** who should be part of the creation process. When effectively integrated, SOPs create a robust framework that supports high-quality, reliable and innovative service delivery. By focusing on these steps, organizations can develop SOPs that support a culture of excellence, ensuring that exceptional service becomes the norm rather than the exception. Hére are the steps to develop effective and relevant SOP's.

Identify Moments of Truth

Identify the main client touchpoints along the entire client journey, the 'Moments of Truth'. Include hereby the virtual touchpoints. Look for opportunities to wow the client. For example, in a hotel, two primary touchpoints are the first and last interactions with the client, namely check-in and check-out.

Document Key Touchpoints

Once the main touchpoints are identified, the next step is to document them in detail. SOPs should be clear, concise and easy to follow. They should outline a step-by-step procedure, including any necessary tools or resources and specify the roles and responsibilities of team members. Visual aids such as flowcharts, images and diagrams can enhance understanding. It is important to empower employees to make decisions and take initiative within the framework of SOPs. This fosters a sense of ownership, accountability and motivation. At the end, SOPs should not be so rigid that employees become robotic. Some tools that can be used include:

CHAPTER V: DEVELOPING OPERATING PROCEDURES

5.1 Standard Operating Procedures (SOP's)

- Checklists and guides help employees adhere to SOPs and service standards. Checklists provide a quick reference to ensure that no steps are missed and that each interaction meets the required standards. They are particularly useful in complex or high-pressure situations.

- Technology and automation play a pivotal role in enhancing the service experience. Technology can streamline processes, improve efficiency and provide clients with seamless and personalized interactions. It can enhance communication with clients through various channels such as email, chat, social media and mobile apps. Automated systems can handle routine tasks such as appointment scheduling, order processing and follow-up communications. This not only frees up employees to focus on more complex and value-added tasks but also ensures that routine tasks are completed accurately and promptly.

- CRM Systems are essential tools for managing client interactions and data. They provide a centralized platform for tracking client information, preferences and interaction history. CRMs enable personalized service and help build stronger client relationships.

CHAPTER V: DEVELOPING OPERATING PROCEDURES

5.1 Standard Operating Procedures (SOP's)

Training And Implementation

Developing SOPs is only the beginning; effective training and implementation are crucial in the next step. Employees should be trained on the SOPs to understand their importance and how to apply them in their daily tasks. Hands-on training sessions, simulations and role-playing can be particularly effective in reinforcing these procedures. Managers should enforce and remind employees of the SOPs if mistakes are made. Ensuring adherence to SOPs requires **ongoing monitoring and supervision**. Regular mystery checks and performance reviews can help identify any deviations from established procedures. Addressing these issues promptly through direct feedback, additional training or corrective measures ensures that standards are maintained. Ultimately, consistency in service delivery builds trust and credibility with clients.

Collecting and Analyzing Client Feedback

Collecting client feedback is invaluable for maintaining consistency. Regularly gathering feedback through surveys, reviews and direct interactions provides insights into how well service standards are being met. Analyzing this feedback helps to identify patterns and areas for improvement in the SOPs. Consistency in SOPs does not mean rigidity. Organizations should strive for continuous improvement by regularly reviewing and refining their service processes and standards. SOPs are living documents that need to be reviewed periodically. This iterative approach ensures that services remain relevant and continue to meet evolving client needs and expectations.

CHAPTER V: DEVELOPING OPERATING PROCEDURES

5.2 Example Of Standard Operating Procedure

The following example is an SOP for a telephone reservation agent of a high-end luxury hotel. It illustrates the different steps, the level of detail and above all how to create a true delight for the client.

Scenario

Situation: The phone is ringing, a guest is willing to make a reservation.

1. A prompt answer is given: aim max. 3 rings or about 10 seconds. The responsiveness is handled by a dedicated, trained employee with a specific order of backup.

a. Back office: Reservations agent
b. Back office: Guest Relations agent (backup)
c. Back office: Front Desk agent (backup)

The incoming call can be taken in a proper area without disturbance. Foresee no disturbance of background noise, no disturbance to the front of the house operations or staff availability, no disturbance by loud and continuous ringing in the reception area, no disturbance by loud speaking on the phone in the reception area.

2. The standard greeting is: "Good morning/Good afternoon/... (greeting), Hotel X, my name is (your name), how may I help you?" Speak in a clear, well-paced, positive and friendly voice.

3. The communication happens in the desired language of the guest which has to be clarified upfront, alternatively in English. The operator may suggest to transfer the call to a colleague, alternatively call back, for a specific foreign language if support so required and available at once or within the shortest delay. Never put somebody on hold for more than 30 seconds.

4. Write down the caller's name in the reservation system in order to use it whenever suitable during the call. Check if the guest already has a profile or stayed before.

CHAPTER V: DEVELOPING OPERATING PROCEDURES

5.2 Example Of Standard Operating Procedure

Above all, listen to what the caller is looking for. Take your time to be complete. The agent captures and inputs the information below directly into the reservation system, (see checklist)
- Rooms and dates, number of guests
- All guest names, including children and age (reverify for correct spelling)
- Previous stays if applicable (retrieve profile if there is one already)
- Contact details (mobile phone and e-mail)
- Purpose of visit: specific objectives, interests, activities or programs
- Special requests in room, food/dietary or others
- Transport arrangements
- Time of arrival expected
- Restaurant, wellness, activity reservations
- Payment terms, cancellation policy, deposit policy
- Credit card number to guarantee reservation and extras if applicable

6. Take time to excel in service, go the extra mile. Guide the client in finding answers based on open-ended question techniques, which will provide you with a maximum amount of information. What is the purpose of your visit (hiking, wellness, gastronomy, etc.)? What are your room preferences (pillow, minibar, amenities, surprises, etc.)? Potentially, closed questions. Would you like to have the same room as last time? (Answer: Yes or No)

7. Read back the relevant points of information at the end of the conversation in order to confirm the information.

8. Upsell proposal, propose several adequate alternatives based on the guest information, needs and performance; clearly explain the rates and fees of each option.

9. If you need to verify information to assist the caller, place the call on hold. Do not keep the caller on the line as they will be able to hear all other conversations. Always make sure to tell the caller you are placing the call on hold. When you retrieve the caller from holding, thank them for waiting. Never put somebody on hold for more than 30 seconds.

10. Ask if there is anything else you can do for the caller before closing the call.

11. Confirm if the client would like to receive information by e-mail on specific interest he or she indicated, that might be of interest for the future stay(s).

CHAPTER V: DEVELOPING OPERATING PROCEDURES

5.2 Example Of Standard Operating Procedure

12. Inform the caller on the next steps:
- A confirmation will be sent out by email within 1 hour, together with inspirational flyers according to the guest's preferences.
- If applicable, a dedicated employee will reach out by phone to further detail and ascertain the specific programs and activities as stated during a call.

13. Thank the caller for the reservation and wish him a sincere goodbye greeting.

14. Allow the caller to hang up first as this ensures they have finished the conversation.

15. Profile verification: link an existing or a create new profile, tick the right labels or codes in the system. Enter accurately all details in respective systems.

16. Send the confirmation within 1 hour after the call as per standards.

Expected outcomes of these SOP's

- Personalization: Use the caller's name and language, profile verification, preferences. This makes the clients feel more important and recognizes their loyalty.
- Inspirational: Enhanced positivism, focus on experience, engagement, questions. Do not be functional in the tasks, but above all transmit positivism in the communication.
- Efficiency: No waiting, no disturbance, no interruptions, right flow and pace. Be efficient and effective for both the guest and the organization. Demonstrate competence.
- Data Management: Deep-dive into the details, register the data correctly. Accuracy for future client engagement is key.

CHAPTER V: DEVELOPING OPERATING PROCEDURES

5.2 Example Of Standard Operating Procedure

Extra tips

When writing Standard Operating Procedures (SOPs) in a client-facing environment, several practical factors must be considered to ensure clarity, consistency, compliance, efficiency and maximal client satisfaction. Creating effective SOPs in a client-facing environment requires time, collaboration and is a thoughtful approach, it is surely not a quick and dirty work. Here are the key considerations and best practices for writing effective SOPs:

- Know who will be reading and using the SOPs is crucial, the audience includes employees who interact directly with clients. Understanding their needs, skills and challenges will help in tailoring the SOPs to be practical, user-friendly and comprehensible.
- Explain why the procedure is necessary and what are the expected outcomes. This clarity helps to ensure that employees understand the importance of following the SOPs and how it impacts their work and the client relationship.
- Involvement of key stakeholders, including frontline employees and managers, in the development of SOPs ensures that the procedures are realistic and practical.
- The language used in SOPs should be simple, straightforward and free of jargon. Employees need to understand the procedures without ambiguity. Visual aids such as flowcharts, diagrams and screenshots can enhance understanding.
- SOPs should be easily accessible to all employees, whether in print or digital format. Implementing a robust document control system ensures that employees always have access to the latest versions of SOPs; changes hereby are well communicated.
- SOPs must align with relevant regulatory and legal requirements, especially in industries such as healthcare, finance, telecommunications and food industry. Ensuring that SOPs are up-to-date with current laws and regulations protects the company from legal risks and builds client trust.
- SOP's should be elaborative on how employees should handle various client interactions to maintain a high level of service. This can be by breaking down complex processes into manageable steps.
- Clearly defining roles and responsibilities within SOPs ensures that employees know what is expected of them and improves accountability.
- SOPs should reflect the company's culture and values, reinforcing the importance of client-centricity and high standards of service.

CHAPTER V: DEVELOPING OPERATING PROCEDURES

5.2 Example Of Standard Operating Procedure

- SOP's leave room for freedom, not to become robotic employees. SOP's leave ownership to respond to unexpected situations and who to contact for assistance.
- Utilizing technology can enhance the effectiveness of SOPs.
- Write SOP's in the interest of the clients and not in the ease of work for the staff or internal processes.
- When writing SOP's, go the extra mile, beyond what is common industry practice.
- ....

CHAPTER VI: MANAGING COMPLAINTS

6.1 Managing complaints

In any client-facing environment, complaints are inevitable. How these are managed differs and can significantly impact client satisfaction and loyalty. This chapter explores strategies for managing client complaints, conflict resolution techniques, turning negative experiences into positive outcomes and creating an open culture of accepting feedback. With help of effective complaint handling, organizations can exceed client expectations, build lasting relationships and address immediate issues that leads to a culture of continuous improvement and exceptional service.

Who likes to get a complaint? No one? That would be sad! Don't miss the opportunity to become better. Above all, the key issue with complaints is to install a culture in which complaints are accepted at all levels of the organization. No one is perfect and things will go wrong. Accepting to have made a mistake or an organizational failure is not easy to accept for some hierarchic cultures, for example Japanese, Russian or Chinese, but is a first step to resolution. Some employees might not even report complaints out of the fear of bad consequences or missing out on incentives. Having a culture of complaint handling goes along with a clear mandate and interest from the top management to take complaints seriously and to have the required processes in place to deal with them. As such, any organization should have a culture of exploration by an iterative interrogation 'why why why why why' something happened, like the Kaizen principle at Toyota cars to foster constant improvement. It might be that the complaints addressed by the client are much wider and deeper than they appear on the surface. The client sees the top of the iceberg but does not formulate the real problem behind it. By exploring the content of a complaint, the business owner should understand underlying issues. That is why it is crucial to have an internal reporting tracking system that clusters and tracks all issues centrally. Ideally, staff should take the time and be encouraged to report each complaint. For example, in a restaurant:

- "Slow service despite many empty places" potentially means a waste of resources, inefficiencies in kitchen or service, motivational issues, staff absenteeism, etc.
- "Rude staff" potentially means wrong attitude, bad training, unmotivated staff, no values, badly threated staff, wrong hiring process, toxic culture, etc.
- "Items not being available despite being on the menu" potentially means wrong inventories, bad suppliers, problems in kitchen to deliver, technical issues, etc.
- "Too pricy" potentially means low service, not price competitive to similar restaurants, unprofessional to deliver quality, not cost efficient, bad processes, etc.

CHAPTER VI: MANAGING COMPLAINTS

6.2 The L-E-A-R-N Method

The most known technique for complaint management in a client-facing environment is the L-E-A-R-N method. There are five steps to consider in this method:

Listen

Active listening is the first step in managing client complaints. Clients need to feel heard and understood. When a complaint is received, give the client your full attention, listen without interrupting and acknowledge their concerns. Let the client ventilate his temper within the limits of the acceptable.

Empathize

Empathy is crucial in complaint management. Put yourself in the client's shoes and express understanding of their frustration or disappointment. Phrases like "I understand how you feel" or "I can see why this is upsetting" can help calm the situation and show the client that their feelings are valid. This demonstrates empathy and respect.

Apologize

A sincere apology can go a long way in diffusing a tense situation. Acknowledge the mistake or issue, apologize for the inconvenience caused and assure the client that you are committed to resolving the problem. A genuine apology demonstrates accountability and a commitment to client satisfaction.

React

Once the client's concerns have been acknowledged, investigate the issue thoroughly. Gather all relevant information, identify the root cause of the problem and determine the best course of action. Keep the client informed about the progress and expected resolution time, so the client understands the issue won't happen anymore.

Now

Offer practical and timely solutions to address the client's concerns. Whenever possible, involve the client in the resolution process by discussing potential solutions and agreeing on the best way forward.

CHAPTER VI: MANAGING COMPLAINTS

6.2 The L-E-A-R-N Method

This collaborative approach ensures that the client's needs are met and fosters a sense of partnership. A client might be surprised by the sudden overwhelming attention for the issue if the business owner or superior manager took the time to deal with it as it was the highest priority.

Remark to follow up with the clients after the resolution to ensure they are satisfied with the outcome and to reinforce the positive experience. The follow-up helps to rebuild trust and demonstrates ongoing commitment to the client's satisfaction.

CHAPTER VI: MANAGING COMPLAINTS

6.3 The Don'ts With Complaints

At the other side of the spectrum, there are as well several "don'ts" or pitfalls to avoid when answering to client complaints.

- Cheap excuses: "It was the busiest day of the year and we are 3 people short" Giving excuses equals apologizing for being bad and admitting it. It even could reveal other untouched issues that the organization is dealing with. Excuses only raise more questions about the competency of running the business properly. Secondly, getting complaints is not an issue of having right or wrong so don't provide feedback on feedback.
- No ownership: "It is not my business, however I will tell the manager". "I am just the operator, don't blame me." Avoiding responsibility is interpreted as not providing a listening ear. The client may think he is speaking to a wall or his comments will be in vain.
- No real compensation: Depending on the severity of the complaint, compensation might be adequate. If the damage is significant, the compensation should be at least equal, ideally more. Be generous and overwhelming, not stingy.
- Impossible to help: "I am sorry but we cannot help you". For every reasonable request, there should be a reasonable answer. Especially when working in a more luxury environment where everything is possible. Most clients know what is possible and what is not. A 'no' means another deception and closes the door for future purchases.
- Over-automation and standardization: There is no value in a trained standardized (robotic) answer whereas there is value in a complaint. If no effort is taken by the business, the incentive to complain disappears and valuable information will not be revealed. Remain human at all time.

CHAPTER VI: MANAGING COMPLAINTS

6.4 Conflict resolution

Conflict resolution is an essential skill in client-facing environments. Effective conflict resolution techniques help to **de-escalate** situations, to find mutually beneficial solutions, and to maintain positive relationships. Here are concrete tips.

Avoid emotions

Conflicts contain emotion and emotions contain danger to escalation. Take out the tension by staying calm and professional. Maintaining composure is essential during conflicts. Stay calm, keep your emotions in check, and approach the situation with a professional demeanor. This helps prevent the situation from escalating and sets a positive tone for resolution. Neutral language can help de-escalate conflicts and facilitate constructive dialogue. Avoid blaming or accusatory language and focus on describing the issue objectively. Use phrases like "I noticed that..." or "It seems that..." to keep the conversation neutral and focused on the problem. Do not refer to any person. In more complex or entrenched conflicts, **mediation** may be necessary. Help of third party, ideally a superior in the organization, can facilitate dialogue, clarify misunderstandings, and guide the parties towards a resolution. Mediation can be particularly effective in resolving conflicts where emotions run high or where previous attempts at resolution have failed.

Collaborate

Understanding the underlying cause of the conflict is crucial for effective resolution. Engage in open dialogue with all parties involved to gather information and identify the root cause. This understanding forms the basis for finding a fair and lasting solution. Engage as well on the **same hierarchical level** and not as a subordinate. The Ritz-Carlton hotels use the saying 'Gentlemen serving gentlemen'. Look for areas of agreement and common ground. This can help build rapport and create a foundation for resolving the conflict. Acknowledge any valid points made by the client and express a willingness to work together to find a solution. Brainstorm potential solutions with the client. Creative solutions are great, so think! Be open-minded and consider multiple options or solutions. Propose options and work towards a mutually acceptable solution. This collaborative approach fosters a sense of shared responsibility and partnership.

CHAPTER VI: MANAGING COMPLAINTS

6.4 Conflict resolution

Acknowledging

Prompt acknowledgment of the issue is the first step to de-escalate. Quickly recognizing and addressing the problem shows the client that their concerns are taken seriously and that the organization is committed to resolving the issue. Use the negative experience as a learning opportunity. Conduct a thorough analysis to understand what went wrong and why. Implement changes to prevent similar issues from occurring in the future. Sharing these improvements with the client demonstrates a commitment to continuous improvement and client satisfaction. Thank the client for bringing the issue to your attention and for their patience during the resolution process. Expressing gratitude reinforces the positive outcome and shows that the organization values client feedback. Follow up with the client after the resolution to ensure they are satisfied with the outcome and to reinforce the positive experience. This follow-up helps rebuild trust and demonstrates ongoing commitment to the client's satisfaction. These are all steps of the LEARN method.

CHAPTER VI: MANAGING COMPLAINTS

6.5 The Service Recovery Paradox

Client complaints, while challenging, are opportunities to improve the service and build **stronger relationships as before**. The service recovery paradox is a phenomenon where clients who experience a problem and receive a satisfactory resolution become more loyal than clients who never experienced a problem. Meaning, the manner of dealing with the issue impressed the client above expectations. In order to reach such a result, one must go above and beyond in resolving the issue. Offer more than just a solution to the immediate problem; provide additional value to the client. This could include exclusive complimentary services, discounts or personalized attention. At the end, the event should be memorable. How to do this? Personalization is key to effective service recovery. Tailor the resolution to the specific needs and preferences of the client, hereby using creativity. This shows that the organization values them as individuals and is committed to their individual satisfaction. Secondly, a proper service recovery demonstrates sincere empathy and competence which leads to trust.

CHAPTER VII: THE FUTURE OF CLIENT SERVICE

7.1 Emerging Trends In Serving Clients

The future of service excellence is shaped by emerging trends, technological advancements and evolving client expectations. Organizations must embrace a client-centric mindset, invest in technology and innovation and foster a culture of continuous improvement to stay ahead. Digital experiences play a crucial role in the entire client journey, offering opportunities for real-time interaction, personalization and seamless integration. As the experience economy gains prominence, creating memorable and engaging experiences becomes essential to achieving business success. By understanding and adapting to these dynamics, organizations can ensure their business model remains outstanding and future-proof.

Client expectations are evolving. In the age of instant gratification, clients expect quick and efficient support. They want their issues resolved promptly, their questions answered without delay and a seamless integration across all touchpoints in their journey. Whether they are interacting with a website, mobile app or client support, they want a consistent and integrated experience. This expectation is driving the adoption of omnichannel support, integrated platforms, adoption of AI and chatbots, which provide instant support and handle routine queries in real-time. Omnichannel service delivery ensures that clients receive consistent and integrated experiences regardless of the channel they choose. Currently, some industries struggle to deliver consistency and to adapt their business model to omnichannel services. In particular banks try to push digitalization through at cost of closing local bank offices and in-person contact, simply out of cost-saving perspective. This push towards digitalization still encounters resistance from older generations or against more complex inquiries. It is difficult to find a right balance in the speed of digital transition, but change is a must.

Digitalization and digital experiences are now an integral part of the client journey, encompassing a range of touchpoints such as websites, mobile apps, social media, self-service kiosks or online support. Each touchpoint offers opportunities to engage and delight clients, but as well provide other opportunities among which data analytics with or without help of AI, real-time interactions to respond promptly to client inquiries and client issues at a low cost, personalized content, product recommendations, etc. Augmented and virtual reality are transforming client service by providing immersive experiences. For example, clients can visualize products in their own environment using AR, or receive virtual tours and demonstrations through VR, enhancing their engagement and satisfaction for example by Apple Vision Pro or iGlasses.

CHAPTER VII: THE FUTURE OF CLIENT SERVICE

7.1 Emerging Trends In Serving Clients

Internet of Things connects devices and can provide real-time updates, predictive maintenance alerts or personalized recommendations; hereby creating a more responsive and proactive service environment. An example is the connectivity of your car to a mobile app. Although it seems to be far away, it is not. Take the example of mobile payment systems that have found their way up to the smallest café or restaurant in the street. We cannot imagine a world without technology and digitalization. With further **democratization of solutions**, we expect enhancements in the digital client journey and the removal of internal manual processes. It is an undoubtable bright win-win story.

Clients are increasingly valuing sustainability and corporate social responsibility (CSR). Organizations that integrate these values into their service strategies can enhance client loyalty and attract new clients who prioritize ethical considerations. Clients expect companies to be honest and upfront about their products, services and policies. For example, this expectation might be driving the adoption of blockchain technology, though still at early stage, which can provide secure and transparent records of client interactions, secure payment processing or data privacy management.

In addition, personalization is no longer a luxury; it is a necessity. Clients expect interactions that are tailored to their individual needs and preferences. This expectation is driving the use of data analytics and AI to create personalized experiences that resonate with clients on a deeper level. More and more organizations will know you as good as Facebook and Instagram does. Despite the rise of A.I. and technological solutions, clients still value the human touch. They want to feel understood and valued in their interactions with organizations. This expectation is driving the need for support teams to develop strong interpersonal skills and demonstrate empathy in their interactions, which refers to emotional intelligence. Emotions matter. Training staff to develop high emotional intelligence can lead to more empathetic and effective client service, fostering stronger client relationships. This becomes even more important in the perspective of 'emotional branding'. These phenomena increase brand value by using the right storytelling, message or design to reach target audience.

CHAPTER VII: THE FUTURE OF CLIENT SERVICE

7.1 Emerging Trends In Serving Clients

The luxury fashion brand Chanel is a great example of a luxury brand with a high emotional intelligence, driven primarily by elements of brand expertise, quality of products and client service experience. Chanel ranks top for its client service experience and therefore excels as a brand and in its' financial performance. A result of emotional intelligence is the pro-active service, involving the anticipation of client needs and addressing them before they become issues.

This trend is gaining momentum as organizations leverage predictive analytics and artificial intelligence (AI) to foresee and mitigate potential problems. Overall, emotional intelligence (EI) in client service focuses on understanding and managing emotions to improve interactions.

The emotions can be enhanced by the experiences. We are living in an experience economy that emphasizes creating memorable and engaging experiences for clients. This shift from goods and services to experiences reflects changing client priorities and expectations. Luxury retail brands have well understood this concept of experience, the value of a store visit goes beyond the product or service itself to the entire client journey. They install in their stores workshops, community events, but as well pieces of art, bars with lounges, catering facilities to please their UHNWI (Ultra-High-Net-Worth-Individuals) clientele. Meanwhile Starbucks or McDonald's offer outlets with a strong immersive brand experience. Organizations can differentiate themselves by focusing on the emotional aspects which involve designing interactions or interiors that are not only efficient but also recognizable, enjoyable and memorable. Effective storytelling and a compelling brand narrative can enhance the client experience. By communicating their values, mission and unique story, organizations can connect with clients on a deeper level.

CHAPTER VII: THE FUTURE OF CLIENT SERVICE

7.2 Preparing The Digital Future Of Service Excellence

The most critical question is to understand how to apply the principles out of past chapters in a practical manner and to be a weaponed for contemporary and future trends. Considering the ongoing digital trends, it goes without saying that service excellence will go hand in hand with technological solutions, but at the same time without losing the benefits of human contact. The ability to deliver personalized interactions at scale and at a cost-effective method, such as using data and advanced analytics in an omni-channel environment to target the needs, is becoming a cornerstone of service excellence and requires organizations to invest in technologic innovation while at the same time still investing in human capital such as training programs.

The question is how to design a digital service excellence framework? The best answer is to start with the question 'Who is my client?' (buyer personas). Companies must first understand what matters most to their clients before they can design an engaging client experience. Hereby clients can support to design the experience process based on their feedback and collected data across the client touchpoints.

Client data collection is complex for larger organizations with several departments and offices worldwide. For any organization, it is essential to aim for an **overarching IT strategy** across the organization and to map the different omnichannel journeys of clients from A to Z, not to work in silos! For example, avoid fragmentation of client data by a 'spaghetti' of endless different IT-systems and back-end interfaces. Organizations require one single comprehensive data strategy. Fortunately, I observe across industries the trend to move towards data warehousing, data platforms or data lakes as a single source of all data on clients, agents, product performance, surveys and other information sources. I believe as well smaller organizations, SME's, are going to adopt one central data (or CRM) system. Data governance or IT architecture are essential and can be potentially complimented by an ecosystem of industry partners and not to forget A.I! Undoubtedly IT is going to be backbone for the omnichannel service experience to an extend that we cannot even imagine today!

Once the data structure is set in place, it becomes a matter of selecting the right client satisfaction measurement tools per department, as well as other performance indicators and to create accountability and ownership for constant improvements. That is what service excellence is about!

CHAPTER VII: THE FUTURE OF CLIENT SERVICE

7.2 Preparing The Digital Future Of Service Excellence

Therefore, organizations must embrace a culture of continuous improvement that relies on client feedback loops to identify areas for enhancement, install agile methodologies to quickly respond to changing client needs and support processes, update ongoing training and development for the support teams, promote innovation and exploration of new ideas and finally re-install or calibrate client-oriented performance metrics, measuring again improvements on client performance. It is a never-ending loop. Organizations should include metrics or KPIs that reflect the emotional and experiential aspects of client service, such as client delight and emotional engagement and make it accountable to the level of the employee, giving him the ownership to service excellence.

All these measures can only be achieved when the senior leadership team decides to embrace a client-centric mindset, place the client at the center of all decisions and allocate the budgets. At the end, digitalization will be a differentiator in service excellence and become part of the brand value.

CHAPTER VIII: BEST PRACTISES

8.1 Concrete Examples

This overview of successful companies that cherish and adopted a client-oriented culture, should be inspirational for all business owners. It demonstrates that even the big giants consider the importance of service excellence. All listed companies exemplify one of the learnings of the book.

Amazon

Amazon's relentless focus on client service is a cornerstone of its success. They prioritize client satisfaction through fast delivery, a user-friendly interface and exceptional client support. Amazon's ability to handle massive volumes while maintaining high service standards showcases the power of leveraging technology and logistics to meet client expectations. Amazon steers clients to the channels that are best suited to their preferences while also offering digital live interactions and company-initiated contact. Clients still often seek out a live agent on the phone. Despite being a digital leader, Amazon has designed an **omnichannel client-care strategy** in which live agents still figure prominently to handle by phone complex requests, demonstrate empathy and resolve issues quickly on a mass scale.

Zappos

Zappos, an online shoe and clothing retailer, is famous for its client service. Their company culture emphasizes delivering happiness, with a no-questions-asked return policy and a commitment to making every client interaction positive. Zappos' client service approach proves that investing in a **positive work culture** can translate into exceptional client experiences.

Ritz-Carlton

The Ritz-Carlton hotel chain is synonymous with luxury service. Their "Gold Standards" guide every employee to anticipate and fulfill guests' needs proactively. The motto **"We are Ladies and Gentlemen serving Ladies and Gentlemen"** reflects their commitment to service excellence, making Ritz-Carlton a benchmark in the hospitality industry.

CHAPTER VIII: BEST PRACTISES

8.1 Concrete Examples

Apple

Apple's focus on client experience is evident in their product design and client support. The **Apple Store experience**, both in-person and online, is designed to be seamless and user-friendly. Their Genius Bar provides personalized tech support, reinforcing Apple's commitment to exceptional client service.

Nordstrom

Nordstrom, a leading fashion retailer, is known for its client-centric policies, such as a famously generous return policy and personalized shopping experiences. Nordstrom **empowers its employees** to go above and beyond to satisfy clients, demonstrating that trust in staff can lead to superior service.

Southwest Airlines

Southwest Airlines distinguishes itself with friendly and efficient service. Their **employee-first culture** translates into better client experiences, as happy employees are more likely to deliver excellent service. Southwest's transparency and client-friendly policies, like no change fees, build strong client loyalty.

Four Seasons

The Four Seasons hotel chain excels in providing personalized, high-quality service. Their attention to detail and commitment to creating unique guest experiences make them a leader in the luxury hospitality industry. The Four Seasons' service philosophy, "The Golden Rule," emphasizes **"treating others as they wish to be treated"**, inspiring other organizations to prioritize empathy and respect in their service delivery.

Chanel

Chanel invests heavily in **training and developing** its employees to ensure they can provide the highest level of service. This includes training in client service, product knowledge and understanding the brand's values and history. Employees are encouraged to build strong relationships with clients, fostering loyalty and satisfaction.

CHAPTER VIII: BEST PRACTISES

8.1 Concrete Examples

Hermès

Hermès is renowned for its uncompromising commitment to quality. The brand's products are handcrafted using the finest materials, ensuring that each item meets the highest standards. This dedication to quality demonstrates a deep respect for the client and their desire for long-lasting, premium products. Hermès provides **highly personalized services** to its clients. This includes bespoke creations, custom fittings and personalized shopping experiences. By offering tailored services, Hermès ensures that each client feels valued and receives products and experiences that meet their unique preferences.

IKEA

The in-store experience is designed to be **engaging and enjoyable**, with room displays, restaurant facilities and kids' playgrounds. As well IKEA's commitment to sustainability resonates with environmentally conscious consumers, enhancing brand loyalty.

LEGO

Lego is renowned for its high-quality, durable and innovative toys. Lego products are designed to be both fun and educational, appealing to both children and parents. The company fosters a **strong community** through events, online platforms and loyalty programs.

AIRBUS

Airbus is at the forefront of aviation technology, ensuring safety, efficiency and comfort in air travel. The company provides extensive support and maintenance services to its airline clients. Airbus is committed to **reducing its environmental impact**, which is increasingly important to clients and stakeholders.

CHAPTER VIII: BEST PRACTISES

8.2 Selection of Professional Experiences

As a management consultant, I have had the privilege of engaging with organizations across the globe, spanning a diverse range of industries. My work has covered a broad spectrum of areas including service excellence, client experiences, professional training and development programs, corporate culture and performance optimization. These projects have not only provided a deep understanding of various business dynamics but have also offered invaluable personal experiences that underscore the themes explored in this book.

Banking industry

In the realm of banking, I have been involved in several projects focused on enhancing the client experience. One particularly illustrative case involved a bank's tele-support team, which was subjected to a stringent Key Performance Indicator (KPI) reducing the average call duration to below two minutes in average. This KPI was implemented to streamline operations and reduce costs. However, it led to unintended consequences.

The pressure to keep calls brief often resulted in incomplete issue resolution and frustrated clients. Of course, neither the banks' tele-operators were happy with this unneeded stress and the impossibility to provide the service they would desire to give. Many clients found themselves dissatisfied, receiving rapid responses that lacked sufficient detail. This dissatisfaction drove them to seek further assistance through various channels: visiting local branches, contacting their account managers via email, checking information through mobile apps and even calling the helpline again in hopes of connecting with a different agent. This multi-channel approach to seeking resolutions not only increased operational costs but also degraded the overall client experience.

The issue reflects a deeper problem highlighted in a McKinsey & Company study titled "Client First: Personalizing the Client-Care Journey" (2019). The study documented a scenario where a financial services firm faced a high volume of repeat calls. For every 100 client issues, they received over 160 follow-up calls. This pattern was driven by clients who, unsatisfied with initial responses, would repeatedly contact the firm, hoping for a different outcome from different agents. This behavior underscores a critical flaw: the absence of a consistent and effective resolution strategy.

CHAPTER VIII: BEST PRACTISES

8.2 Selection of Professional Experiences

The crux of the problem, as observed, lies in the cultural leadership within the organization of the bank. There appeared to be a discrepancy between the company's stated objective of placing the client at the heart of its operations and the actual execution of this goal. This top-down decision lacked the true commitment to service excellence. Instead, it fostered an environment where operational levels were deprived of ownership and accountability. This was further enhanced by senior management's detachment from frontline operational realities; briefly ivory towers really exist in large banks. A more engaged leadership approach, such as spending time in branches or call centers to directly observe client interactions, could have provided critical insights and facilitated more effective service improvements.

One potential explanation for this gap in service leadership could be the banking industry's overarching focus on profitability, often driven by macroeconomic factors like the national bank interest rates and less by client satisfaction. This focus can overshadow the importance of cultivating a strong service-oriented culture. The perception of banks as financial entities rather than service providers remains a significant challenge in fostering genuine client-centric approaches.

CHAPTER VIII: BEST PRACTISES

8.2 Selection of Professional Experiences

Luxury retail

The luxury retail industry presents a strong emphasis on creating exceptional client experiences through meticulous attention to detail. My engagements with high-end brands in watches, fashion and skincare have revealed an industry deeply committed to crafting unique client journeys.

For instance, one luxury watch brand invested significant resources into developing a signature coffee experience for its clients. This wasn't merely about serving coffee; it was an orchestrated experience involving specially designed mugs bearing the brand's logo, artisanal biscuits or sweets and a carefully narrated backstory. The coffee service was presented on a bespoke plate with an extra glass of water, all following a highly detailed protocol documented with specific guidelines and images. This level of detail extended to the training of staff worldwide, ensuring consistency in delivering this unique experience.

What illustrates the excellence were the discussions around perfecting such a minor aspect of client interaction that often took hours! The aim was to reflect the brand's commitment to aligning every element of the coffee experience with its luxury positioning. This obsession with detail underscores the industry's belief that every moment with the client is an opportunity to reinforce the brand's promise of excellence and to match the quality of its products. I have encountered similar long-lasting workshop sessions on micro-moments in store at other luxury brands.

The luxury retail sector's focuses on creating emotionally memorable experiences. The role of emotions in selling highlights the importance of respecting and delighting clients. The effort to align even the simplest elements, like serving coffee, demonstrates a profound respect for the clientele and a dedication to surpassing their expectations.

CHAPTER VIII: BEST PRACTISES

8.2 Selection of Professional Experiences

Hotel industry

My professional experience in the hotel industry includes conducting numerous mystery visits to premium and luxury hotels. These visits were structured to evaluate both objective criteria, such as operational efficiency and subjective elements, such as storytelling and the quality of staff-client interactions.

During these assessments, I encountered a few hotels where the overall client experience fell significantly short of expectations. The deficiencies were not rooted in the quality of the physical product but in the processes and people – the most essential components of the "3-P model" (Product, Process, People) in a luxury segment. The absence of a strong leadership culture often resulted in unmotivated staff who lacked initiative when not directly supervised. Examples included indifferent reception staff not looking up who is standing in front of them, waiters who were more interested in chatting with colleagues or being on their phone than serving restaurant guests, staff being rude with clients and generally poor attitudes towards maintaining the expected service standards.

These observations pointed to a fundamental issue: a lack of a vision and core values within the organization. Without a clear, unified identity and a strong induction program, employees lacked a sense of ownership and did not consistently embody the brand's values, if there would be any. This gap was further compounded by challenges in recruitment and staff motivation, particularly in less desirable or seasonal locations. While finding suitable staff for hotels can be difficult, especially in remote seasonal areas, there are essential qualities that should not be compromised. Personality traits such as a genuine care for people, helpfulness, communicative abilities and a positive attitude are the minimum for anyone working in hospitality.

CHAPTER VIII: BEST PRACTISES

8.2 Selection of Professional Experiences

Healthcare and wellness industry

The convergence of hospitality principles with healthcare and wellness services is a growing trend, reflecting a shift towards more patient-centered care. The industry approach emphasizes not only the medical treatment but also the overall 360 experience of patients, similar to what one might expect from high-end hotels or luxury resorts.

In my experience with private clinics and wellness centers, the facilities often create luxurious, comforting environments. Admittedly, most of my professional experiences involved expensive private clinics and high ends wellness destinations which aim to go far beyond the public health care services and target mainly high-net-worth-individuals. For example, some of the wellness facilities offered a luxury setting, stunning natural surroundings or expensive art; briefly they were different from the average hospital look.

A striking aspect of the wellness destinations was the level of personalization in patient care. Detailed client profiles were created, including a comprehensive assessment before treatment begins. This allowed for customized programs that cater to the physical and emotional needs of each patient. For example, personalized dietary plans, specific types of exercise and tailored relaxation techniques were common, as well personal follow-up once back home. This maniacal focus on personalization and attention to detail not only enhances the client - provider relationship but also significantly improves the effectiveness of treatments. I believe that this meticulous approach to understanding and addressing each client's unique needs is a hallmark of the industry's commitment to service excellence.

CHAPTER VIII: BEST PRACTISES

8.2 Selection of Professional Experiences

Public services in Switzerland

Switzerland is widely recognized for its exemplary public services, characterized by efficiency, reliability and high standards. For instance, in nearly a decade of living in Switzerland, I have rarely encountered significant service disruptions, such as strikes or train delays, without an immediate and adequate response from the organizations or authorities. This level of responsiveness and the prioritization of public welfare are key components of the country's public service ethos. Swiss public services are known for their streamlined and user-friendly processes.

What surprised me as Management Consultant was the budget the public services made available to even further improve. The mandates that fell under the umbrella of public services were numerous. Some examples could include more appealing and healthier food offer for school canteens, optimizing internal processes to reduce waiting times at the municipal administration, police services on how treat citizens in specific situations, feasibility studies on local reconversion projects, staff trainings for public services, etc.

Overall, the excellence of public services in Switzerland is a testament to the country's commitment to efficiency, quality, innovations, constant improvement and public welfare. The continuous investment in infrastructure, technology and human resources ensures that Swiss public services remain among the best in the world. In my opinion, Switzerland has a genuine culture of service excellence and public welfare.

CHAPTER IX: FINAL WORDS

The simplicity of this book illustrates that delivering service excellence is not a rocket science. At its core, service excellence is about creating memorable experiences for clients, founded on trust, proactive engagement and a profound understanding of their needs and expectations. These elements form the backbone of a superior service experience, where the simplicity of these concepts belies their profound impact.

A deep understanding of clients is not merely a goal; it is a continuous process built through active listening, empathy, accountability and the anticipation of needs. Client understanding is built through active listening, empathy, accountability and the ability to anticipate what clients may require before they explicitly ask. That is why it's important to engage with clients regularly, whether through direct conversations, surveys or feedback forms, to gain insights into their experiences and preferences and hereout commit to continuously improve the measurable performance indicators as there is no state of status quo in service excellence. Such engagement not only helps in fine-tuning services but also in establishing a relationship of mutual respect and understanding. It is a dynamic journey where standing still is not an option; there is always room for improvement and refinement in the quest for service excellence. At the same time, organizations should strive to create a seamless and positive client experience at every virtual and physical touchpoint along the entire client journey.

I believe that in a first place it takes courage as a business leader to prioritize the client experience, such as the reference companies indicated in the book do. The listed companies have in my opinion an inspirational leadership that form the first cornerstone to master service excellence in a client facing environment. Employees who understand the corporate identity, who feel valued and empowered are more likely to provide exceptional service; in addition, recognizing and rewarding outstanding service behaviors reinforces the importance of their actions and motivates staff to consistently strive for excellence what ultimately reflects on the brands value and financial performance (service profit chain).

CHAPTER IX: FINAL WORDS

Effective communication is the second cornerstone of an outstanding service. Communication contains a thousand signals, both verbal or non-verbal and therefor requires the full attention to be well interpreted from the client perspective. Communication also encompasses a two-way interaction, containing eye contact, using appropriate body language and modulating tone of voice, convey warmth, courtesy and professionalism in the wording or over the phone, or through digital platforms. Briefly, an effective client communication clearly identifies an organization, sets themselves apart in a competitive landscape and make a first step towards the long-term relationships with a community of likeminded very loyal clients. High-quality interactions leave clients feeling valued and respected and key to nurturing client loyalty and trust.

To maintain high standards of service, a commitment to continuous improvement is essential. Regularly training and educating staff on best practices, new technologies and evolving customer service trends is a must. Encouraging a culture of feedback, where both clients and employees can share their experiences and suggestions, fosters an environment of constant learning and adaptation. The organization should facilitate the development of staff, so they become more competent, at the same time not losing the authenticity of the individual, the art of being yourself: "master the rules before you break them". Only this approach can lead to personalized service touches, prompt problem resolution, creativity and a genuine willingness to assist clients without becoming robotic. A sincere interest in the client's satisfaction can turn a standard service interaction into an exceptional one.

Beyond people and culture, there is also the aspect of processes. A memorable client journey requires time to engineer. Standard Operating Procedures are designed to facilitate and elevate the interaction with clients, to reduce mistakes and to optimize internal workflows. Organizations should invest a decent time to clarify internal workflows and provide the best client experience.

As an industry professional, I am pleased to see that 'client experience' becomes more and more important within companies. Studies show that allocated budget for client experience flows primarily into employee trainings, followed by defining a vision and implementing the IT tools. Even if many companies have no company culture of client experience yet, business leaders become more and more aware that the 'industry-client-experience-champions' outperform their competitors in revenues, profitability and stock performance.

CHAPTER IX: FINAL WORDS

Secondly, the implementation of IT tools and AI projects, currently still in an early stage, will support organizations to automate repetitive tasks, provide deeper insights into client needs and enable more meaningful client engagements in an omni-channel environment. It will be a game changer for the better of the client and the organization.

In conclusion, service excellence is a multifaceted endeavor that requires a delicate balance of understanding, communication, continuous improvement and efficient processes. It is a journey that demands courage, dedication and a relentless focus on the client. As businesses evolve, the commitment to enhancing client experience will not only drive success but also create lasting relationships built on trust and mutual respect. As we look to the future, the organizations that will thrive are those that prioritize and invest in the client experience, recognizing it as the true differentiator in a crowded marketplace.

REFERENCES

Books

"Service Excellence: Creating Customer Experiences That Build Loyalty" by Ruth N. Bolton

"The Service Profit Chain: How Leading Companies Link Profit and Growth to Loyalty, Satisfaction, and Value" by James L. Heskett, W. Earl Sasser Jr., Leonard A. Schlesinger

"The Customer Rules: The 39 Essential Rules for Delivering Sensational Service" by Lee Cockerell

"The Zappos Experience: 5 Principles to Inspire, Engage, and WOW" by Joseph Michelli

"Client Relationship Management: A Comprehensive Guide to CRM" by Michael Cusumano

Articles

"Measuring Service Quality: SERVQUAL vs. SERVPERF Scales" by P. Parasuraman, Zeithaml, V.A., and Berry, L.L.

"Creating a Culture of Service Excellence" by Leonard Berry and A. Parasuraman

"Employee Engagement and Empowerment in the Workplace" by John P. Meyer and Natalie J. Allen

Websites

Harvard Business Review: Various online accessible articles on customer service, leadership, implementing customer experience analytics and business strategy

Client Gauge: Blog on Financial Services NPS Benchmark

Society for Human Resource Management (SHRM) - Resources on training, development, and employee engagement

REFERENCES

Reports

"2024 Global Customer Service Insights Report" by Microsoft

"Customer Experience Management: The Key to Service Excellence" by McKinsey & Company

Professional references

All professional references relate to the consulting mandates in my role as a Management Consultant for EHL Advisory Services

SPACE FOR PERSONAL NOTES

SPACE FOR PERSONAL NOTES

SPACE FOR PERSONAL NOTES

SPACE FOR PERSONAL NOTES

SPACE FOR PERSONAL NOTES

www.ingramcontent.com/pod-product-compliance
Lightning Source LLC
Chambersburg PA
CBHW070358230526
45471CB00006B/2627